SCHOLASTIC

Multimodal Texts

Digital texts for on-screen literacy lessons

Year 3

Scottish Primary Y4

CREDITS

Author
Liz Miles

Development Editor
Rachel Mackinnon

Assistant Editor
Louise Titley

Series Designers
Micky Pledge and Melissa Leeke

Designer
Micky Pledge

CD-ROM development
CD-ROM developed in association with Infuze Ltd

Acknowledgements
The publishers gratefully acknowledge permission to reproduce the following copyright material:

Hadrian's Villa, *Magnetic bracelets* and *El Niño* websites by Sarah Fleming © 2008, Sarah Fleming (2008, previously unpublished). *The Black Pearl* by Adam Guillain © 2008, Adam Guillain (2008, previously unpublished). *The king who hated to have his hair cut* by Fiona Undrill © 2008, Fiona Undrill (2008, previously unpublished). *Demeter and Persephone* by Clare Robertson © 2008, Clare Robertson (2008, previously unpublished). *Barker!* by Sue Graves © 2008, Sue Graves (2008, previously unpublished). *Voices* by Celia Warren © 2008, Celia Warren (2008, previously unpublished). Extracts from Primary National Strategy's *Primary Framework for Literacy* (2006) www.standards.dfes.gov.uk/primaryframework © Crown copyright. Reproduced under the terms of the Click Use Licence.

Every effort has been made to trace copyright holders for the works reproduced in this book, and the publishers apologise for any inadvertent omissions.

Published by Scholastic Ltd
Villiers House
Clarendon Avenue
Leamington Spa
Warwickshire CV32 5PR
www.scholastic.co.uk

Designed using Adobe InDesign.

Printed in China through Golden Cup Printing Services

1 2 3 4 5 6 7 8 9   8 9 0 1 2 3 4 5 6 7

Text © 2008 Liz Miles
© 2008 Scholastic Ltd

British Library Cataloguing-in-Publication Data
A catalogue record for this book is available from the British Library.
ISBN 978-1407-10014-2

The right of Liz Miles to be identified as the author of this work has been asserted by her in accordance with the Copyright, Designs and Patents Act 1988.

Minimum system requirement:
- PC or Mac with a 4x speed CD-ROM drive and 512MB RAM
- Windows 98/2000/XP or Mac OSX 10.2 or later
- Recommended minimum processor speed 900Mhz
- 16bit sound and graphics card

SCHOLASTIC
www.scholastic.co.uk

SCHOLASTIC
www.scholastic.co.uk

Introduction

What are multimodal and digital texts?

Multimodal texts include at least two of the following:
- written text
- images
- sound
- movement or gesture

Digital texts are those which are electronic.

A digital text does not have to be multimodal and a multimodal text does not have to be digital.

Why teach them?

Multimodal texts are all around us, from picture books to information leaflets, and children are exposed to a large amount of digital information through the internet, computer games, television and so on. The DfES document *Multimodal – ICT – Digital texts* says *The texts children read on screen influence their writing*. These texts and their features need to be studied alongside traditional texts. The Revised Literacy Framework recommends that multimodal or digital elements are incorporated into literacy teaching through the use of digital cameras, sound recording software, presentational software and so on. *Multimodal Texts* allows you and your children to explore these text types in a safe environment.

About the product

The CD-ROM provides:

- Three mini-websites – completely self-contained with live links including photographs, video or audio.
- Video – a short film with narration.
- Animation – moving illustration with voice-over.
- Three stories – one with an alternative ending (decide as a class what the characters chose to do), all fully illustrated with audio versions.
- Playscript – with full audio version to listen to and with individual sound effects to use in whole-class re-enactment.
- Poetry – fully illustrated with audio version.
- Podcast and audio – both with a transcript which scrolls as you listen and a PDF version to print.
- Two sequences of images – listen to the related sound effects by clicking on the buttons.
- Photocopiable pages (also provided in the book).

The book contains detailed teaching ideas based on the CD-ROM texts.

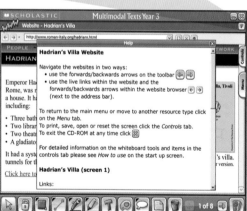

About the CD-ROM

The CD-ROM is installable; follow the text file instructions on the disk to install it on to your system. Once installed, navigate to the program location to open it.

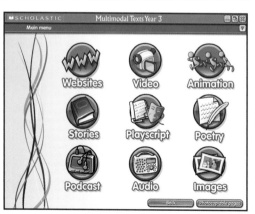

Help

Below are brief guidance notes for using the CD-ROM. For more detailed information see *How to use* on the start-up screen, or see '?' for screen-by-screen help (top right-hand corner of the screen).

Main menu

This screen provides links to all the text types and the photocopiable pages. Click on a text type button to be taken either to the sub-menu or directly to that resource.

SCHOLASTIC
www.scholastic.co.uk

Menu

The menu tab on the right-hand side of the screen allows you to navigate to other areas on the CD-ROM. Click on the tab to open the menu.

Printing

All of the resources are printable. For websites, stories, playscripts, poetry and images there are two print options. You can either print the current screen, including annotations (unless annotations are hidden) or you can print a clean set of the entire resource (every screen). For all other resources the current screen will print with any annotations.

Controls

Click on the controls tab on the right-hand side of the screen to access the Print, Open, Save and Reset-screen buttons.

Whiteboard tools

The CD-ROM comes with its own set of whiteboard tools for use on any whiteboard. These include:

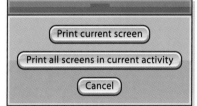

Print (see Printing for more information).

Save all annotations you have made to the texts.

Open – navigate to your saved file to open your annotations.

Reset the page.

Pen tool – draw freehand in three different thicknesses.

Shape tool – add a filled or unfilled circle or square.

Speech / thought bubbles – add a speech or thought bubble.

Text tool – add text using the keyboard.

Rubbish bin – select an annotation and click this button to delete it.

Select tool.

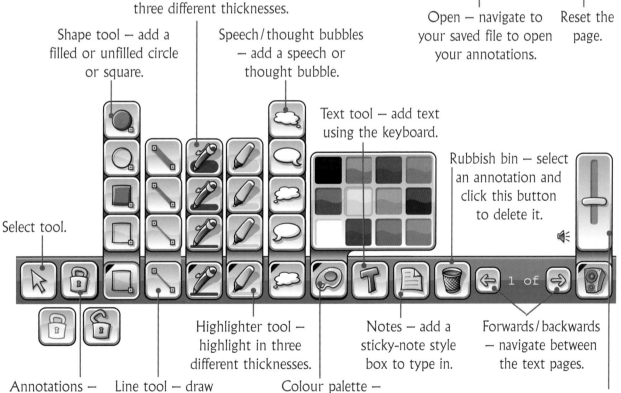

Annotations – on and locked / hidden and locked / unlocked.

Line tool – draw straight lines in three different thicknesses.

Highlighter tool – highlight in three different thicknesses.

Colour palette – select a colour to annotate in.

Notes – add a sticky-note style box to type in.

Forwards / backwards – navigate between the text pages.

Volume – adjust the volume using the slider, or mute by clicking the speaker icon.

Please note – to access buttons on screen, such as playback buttons, the padlock needs to be in the locked position.

Hadrian's Villa

How the text works

- Look at screen 1 of the Hadrian's Villa website. Ask: *What sort of digital text is this?* (A website.) Highlight the web address. Ask: *What does* www *stand for?* (World wide web.) Discuss how all websites have an address. Can the children remember any website addresses that they have used?

- Explore the interactive element of screen 1 by clicking: the image to view the enlarged version and link words (*Click here…*). On screen 3, explore the links by clicking the two images and the words *here* and *Lullingstone Villa*.

- Return to screen 1 and together read the text, then read the text on screen 3. Ask: *What is the subject of screens 1 and 3?* (Hadrian's Roman Villa.) *What is the text type?* Identify and revise the features of report text, including the use of factual descriptions, photographs and captions.

- Discuss the layout and font styles. Ask: *Who is this website for?* Discuss possible audiences, such as school children, adults or tourists.

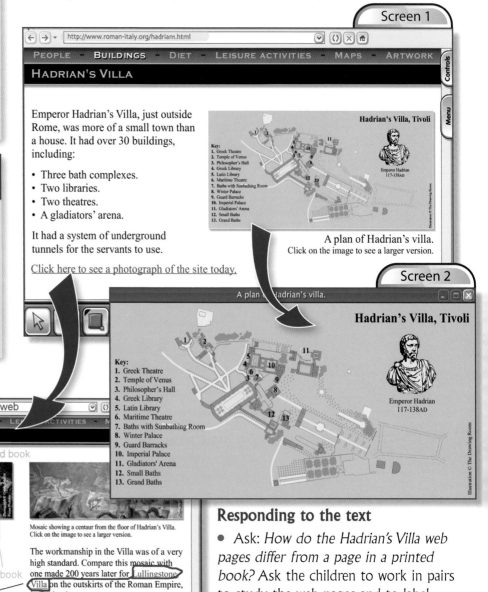

Responding to the text

- Ask: *How do the Hadrian's Villa web pages differ from a page in a printed book?* Ask the children to work in pairs to study the web pages and to label each feature as 'web' if you would only

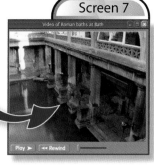
find it on a website (such as: web address, link words, list of contents along the top) and as 'web and book' if you might also find it in a book (for example: captions, photographs, map, list). Ask the children to report their findings to the class.

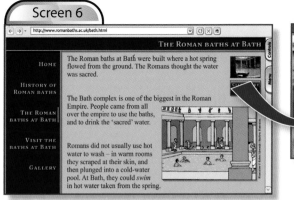

Screen 6

Screen 7

• Ask the children in small groups to explore the pages from the Roman Baths and Mosaics of the Roman Villa at Lullingstone, England websites. Explain that you want them to write notes answering the following questions for each website: *Who is the website for? What is the subject of the website? What are the text types? What interactive features does it have?* Explain that they must back up their answers with examples from the website (for example, quote phrases that tell you what text type it is). Discuss the answers.

• Hold a class debate, followed by a vote on the following: 'The information in the Roman bath video should have been presented as photographs and written text instead.' Ask the class to prepare views both for and against.

Writing activities

• Explain to the children that they are going to use the website information to create a page for a children's non-fiction book on each of the following: (i) Hadrian's Villa and (ii) The Roman baths in Bath.

• Ask the children to work in groups and share out the necessary tasks. Hand out two copies of photocopiable page 34 'Book page plan' to each group and ask them to use one copy to plan each page.

• Explain that they will have to look through the web pages and highlight the information they want to include. Discuss how they can include information from the Roman baths video as text and a picture.

• Discuss how they will need to use two text types (report, plus the explanation on how the baths worked from the video).

• If possible, show the children some books on these or similar subjects and use them to point out the differences between the layout and features of a book and a web page, for example, text in a book is usually black. Revise the use of headings, paragraphs and captions.

• Once they have completed their plans, the children can write and lay out each page on computer. They can draw, scan and position their own illustrations. Text should be written, then revised. Print the pages for display.

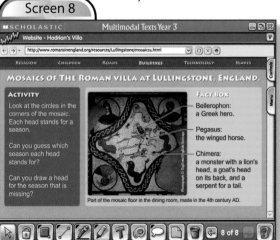

Screen 8

SCHOLASTIC
www.scholastic.co.uk

Whiteboard tools

• Whiteboard tools used on the screen shots include:
▭ Outline box
╲ Line tool
✐ Pen tool
▰ Highlighter
⊤ Text tool
◉ Colours used ○ ● ●

Assessment

• Ask the children to take turns to say which they think is the most useful when looking for information, and why: information books or websites.

References to *100 Literacy Framework Lessons*

• Non-fiction Unit 1 Reports pages 104–106
• Non-fiction Unit 3 Information texts pages 140–141

Photocopiable

• See page 34 or CD-ROM.

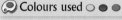

Magnetic bracelets

How the text works

● Look together at screen 1, and ask: *How do we move to the next screen?* (Click on *What to do* in the menu or the *What to do>* button on the screen.) On screen 2, read the text and ask: *What is the main text type?* (Instruction text.) Together identify the text type features (such as: a list of what is needed (screen 1), sequenced list of instructions, diagrams, language written in the imperative, factual description).

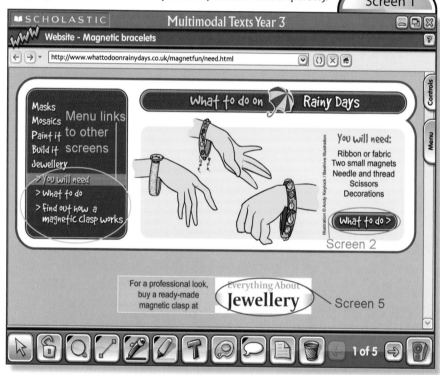

● Together find the link to screen 3 (*Next>*). After reading the text, ask the children to find another working link to a different screen. (*Find out how…*) Ask them to predict what information they would find by clicking on this.

● Explore the link to see if they were right. Identify the text as explanation. Ask: *Is this a page from a different website?* Navigate back and forth between screens 3 and 4 and identify the features that show they are part of the same website (similar web address and layout).

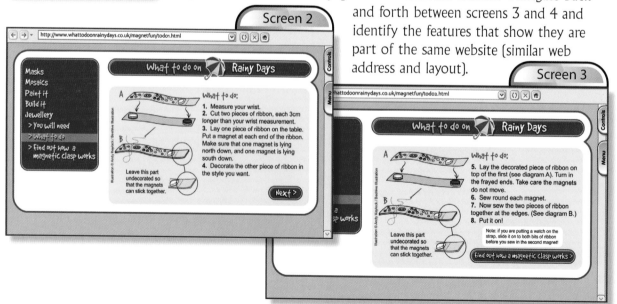

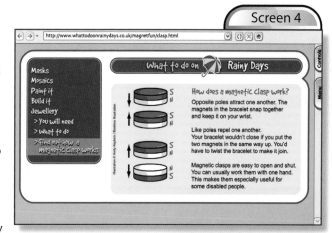

- Return to screen 1 and point to the banner advertisement. Ask: *Why are different colours and fonts used here?* (It is an advert.) *Where do you think the link will take us?*

- Explore the *Everything About Jewellery* link with the children (screen 5). *Is this a page from a different website? What is its purpose?* (Yes. To sell ready-made magnetic clasps.)

- Discuss the features of the online shop website. Note that the links do not work, but prompt children to predict the information they would find if they could click on items such as: *About us, Search, Hook-and-eye clasps.* Ask the children: *What would you click on if you wanted to buy two silver tone barrel magnetic clasps?* (Shopping trolley icon.) Describe the stages that follow or invite volunteers who are familiar with online shops to explain how they work.

Responding to the text

- Tell the children to work in pairs and list the ways in which the website for the online shop is different from the 'How to' website. Ask them to suggest an audience for each (children / jewellery makers). Tell them to focus on details such as the text type and language features, the content (such as pictures), layout (how information is grouped), and design (the font size / styles and colour use). Invite volunteers to point out the different website features on the whiteboard.

- Ask: *Are the features of the online shop website effective?* Discuss the text types (descriptive, persuasive and informative), the graphics and layout. Ask: *Would the website make you want to buy the items? Do you think it is easy to understand? What features would improve the website?* (For example, more pictures.)

- Challenge the children to work out how they would reorganise the information in the online shop to make a leaflet. Explain that, like the website, it must: tell us what it is selling and how the product works; persuade us to buy; show us how to buy. Elicit how the checkout can be replaced with a tear-off order form.

Writing activities

- Hand out photocopiable page 35 'How to… Where to buy…' and ask the children to work in groups to plan and write an instructional web page, for example, how to make a collage or a maquette. They must include a link to a selling website where one of the items needed can be bought, such as glue from an art supplier. After completing their plans, the children can write and lay out each page on a computer. Illustrations can be drawn, scanned and positioned, or clip art uploaded.

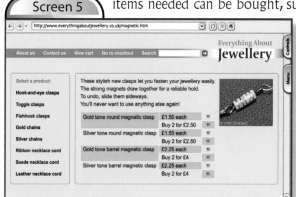

Screen 5

Whiteboard tools

- Whiteboard tools used on the screen shots include:
  - Outline circle
  - Line tool
  - Text tool
  - Colours used ○ ● ●

Assessment

- Ask the children to present their websites to the rest of the class. Identify certain success criteria, such as: *Is there enough information? Will the design attract the reader? Have relevant links been included?*

References to *100 Literacy Framework Lessons*

- Non-fiction Unit 2 Instructions pages 131–132
- Non-fiction Unit 3 Persuasion pages 144–146

Photocopiable

- See page 35 or CD-ROM.

El Niño

How the text works

- Look at screen 1 with the class and ask: *What sort of digital text is this?* Together review the website features that are immediately obvious, for example: website address, *Hot Links*, *Site Index*.

- Ask the children to explore screens 1–2 and highlight all the interactive elements: menu buttons, link buttons to next screen, maps that enlarge, scroll bar.

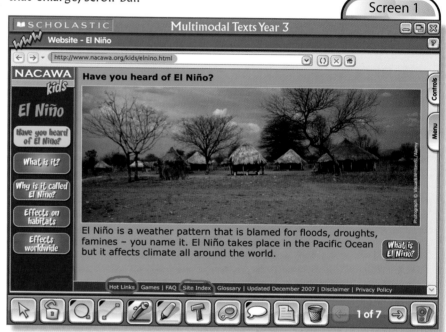

Screen 1

- Invite the children to read the text on all the web pages. Ask: *What is the purpose of the website?* (To describe and explain El Niño.)

- Ask: *What text type is used?* (Report on screens 1–2 and 6–7, with explanation on screen 5.) If necessary, revise the features of report and explanation texts.

- Talk about how the text is organised. Ask: *What features are used to group related information?* (Headings, paragraphs, different font sizes / styles, coloured panels.)

- Is the website for children or adults? (Children.) Point out the informal language (*you name it*), the link to *Games*, and *Kids* in the NACAWA logo and in the website address. Ask: *How might the colours and font styles differ if this was a website for adults?* For example, fewer bright colours, more formal fonts.

- Discuss the maps and photographs. Ask: *Do the maps and photographs add interest to the web pages? Do they provide additional information?* (For example, the map shows us places affected by El Niño.) Ask: *Why is it useful to be able to enlarge the maps?* (Easier to read; as separate pages they can be printed or saved for reference.)

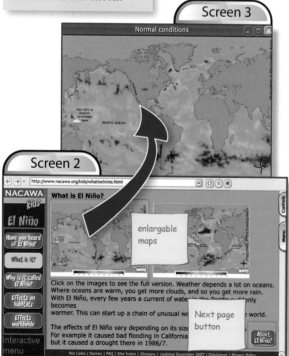

Screen 3

Screen 2

■SCHOLASTIC
www.scholastic.co.uk

Responding to the text

• Prompt the children to describe what sort of information they would expect to find in the site index. What other information might NACAWA kids have on it? Ask them to work in pairs and write a list of links to other screens. Tell them to note down the form each link would take, for example: a link word or a web address embedded in the text for closely related information or a separate icon for different information.

• Ask the children to work in groups and come up with three ideas on how the website could be made more appealing to children, including changes in presentation and additional information, for example, a 3D globe instead of flat map; addition of video clips. Encourage ideas for sound effects and graphics. Invite children to report their ideas to the class.

Writing activities

• Ask the children to work in groups to research another extreme weather type, for example, hurricanes or droughts. Explain that they will use the information to write and design three web pages for children of their own age.

• Give out and talk through photocopiable page 36 'Extreme weather website', outlining the information they might cover on each page, such as: 'Page 1 – What is it?', 'Page 2 – What are its main effects? Which parts of the world does it affect?', 'Page 3 – What causes it?' Remind them to think about appropriate ways of presenting information, for example a dramatic video for a hurricane storm, photographs of a drought. Remind them to note down suitable link buttons and words.

• Ask the groups to share out the tasks, including drawing and scanning their artwork to represent photographs or videos.

• The children can complete their pages on computer, drop in the visual elements and choose suitable fonts and colours. Ensure that links are highlighted even if they are not live.

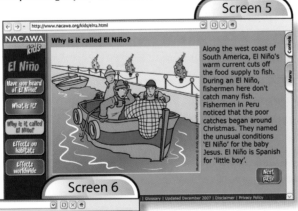

Screen 5

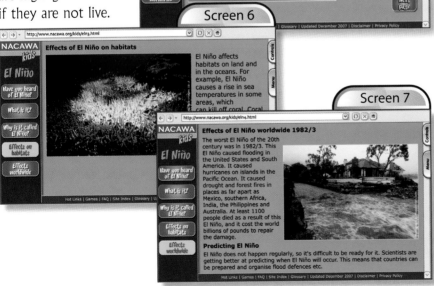

Screen 6

Screen 7

Whiteboard tools

• Whiteboard tools used on the screen shots include:
  ⬜ Outline box
  ✏ Pen tool
  ✐ Highlighter
  ⬆ Text tool
  📄 Sticky notes
  ◎ Colours used ● ●

Assessment

• Ask the children to identify the differences between the El Niño website and an entry in an encyclopedia on El Niño or a similar subject. What features does each have and how do they differ? Ask the children to list their ideas independently, and then discuss as a class.

References to *100 Literacy Framework Lessons*

• Non-fiction Unit 1 Reports pages 104–106
• Non-fiction Unit 3 Information texts pages 140–143

Photocopiable

• See page 36 or CD-ROM.

A day in the life

Objectives

- Strand 2: Identify the presentational features used to communicate the main points in a broadcast.
- Strand 10: Signal sequence, place and time to give coherence.

Differentiation

Support
- Children can focus on the visual element, and draw a sequence of images to represent 'stills' for each scene to be filmed.
Extend
- Children can use a video camera to record their video storyboard.

Cross-curricular activities

Citizenship Unit 4
People who help us
- Invite someone who helps you to the school (such as, a postman, lollipop lady or nurse). Prepare questions in advance so that an audio of a day in the life of that person can be recorded.

Whiteboard tools

- Whiteboard tools used on the screen shots include:
🅣 Text tool
🅠 Colour used ●

How the text works

- Watch the video with the children. Help the children to identify the subject (a woman's first day at work in a dog re-homing centre). *Who do they think the video is for?* (For example: people thinking of working in a dog's home.)

- Ask: *What is the text type?* (First-person recount.) Together identify some of the 'time' words by listening carefully. List the examples they have heard on the board, for example, *about 7 o'clock*, *then* and *next*.

- Watch the video again and ask the children to consider how the passing of time is also shown visually (scene changes; clock-style graphics, such as during Labrador walk; speeded-up film) and through the soundtrack (fast beat music — almost like a clock ticking).

- Consider the camera's viewpoint. Although the text is first person, the camera's viewpoint is third person. Ask: *Would it have been better if the woman had operated the camera, and spoken to it directly, like a video diary?* For example, the speaker in a video diary might say more about how she feels.

- Ask: *Does the visual element provide extra information?* Identify

information that is shown but not mentioned (type of building, dogs had blankets / toys).

- *Other than the narrator, what else do we hear?* Tell the children to list to any sounds they hear apart from the main narrator. Challenge them to note down their purpose. For example, dialogue: Rachel says

📖SCHOLASTIC
www.scholastic.co.uk

'Hi there, lovely to see you,' shows she is friendly; fast-beat music: exciting, sense of a busy day; dogs' echoing barks: atmosphere.

Responding to the text

● Demonstrate noting the content of the video on a timeline, stopping the video and making a note each time a reference to time is heard. Ask the children to complete the timeline, gathering information from both sound and pictures.

● Invite volunteers to hot-seat the woman. One child takes the role of the woman, the other children take it in turns to ask a question about her day, using the

information on their timeline for reference. The person in role must try to recall the information and answer accurately. If they answer incorrectly, it is the questioner's turn to take the hot-seat.

[Fast-moving music throughout. Camera shows narrator arriving at dog's home and walking up drive to door [viewed from driveway].]

Narration: It was my first day at the dog re-homing centre.

[Camera shot from inside shows narrator coming in and greeting friendly manager. We hear the manager saying 'Hi there, lovely to see you.']

Narration: It was my job…

[Camera follows narrator down long corridor to kennels. Sound of barking dogs echoing.]

Narration: I got to work at about 7 o'clock…

Writing activities

● Explain that the children are going to write the opening scenes for a video storyboard entitled 'My day at school'. Tell them to start by completing a timeline of their arrival at school and what they did first.

● Demonstrate how to write a video storyboard, using the video timeline of the dog's home [see box to the left].

● Emphasise the importance of camera and sound directions, as well as the narrative, to give information about the setting, people and atmosphere.

● Hand out photocopiable page 37 'My day at school'. Remind the children to refer to their timeline as they order the events on the storyboard.

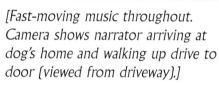

Assessment

● Ask volunteers to share their video storyboards. Encourage the children to take turns to offer suggestions as to how more information can be given about the setting and people, using features from the dog re-homing video, for example atmospheric sound, dialogue, additional visual information / details.

Reference to *100 Literacy Framework Lessons*

● Non-fiction Unit 3 Information texts pages 137–152

Photocopiable

● See page 37 or CD-ROM.

Objectives

● Strand 2: Identify the presentational features used to communicate the main points in a broadcast.
● Strand 9: Use layout, format, graphics and illustrations for different purposes.

Differentiation

Support
● Children can complete instructions on a simpler process, such as 'How to wash your hands properly'.
Extend
● Children can use a digital camera to create a sequence of images, upload them to a computer and add their narration as an audio.

Cross-curricular activities

PE Unit 10
Invasion games
● Ask the children to create an animation to show the instructions for a game.

Whiteboard tools

● Whiteboard tools used on the screen shots include:
⬉ Line tool
T Text tool
◉ Colour used ●

Do plants need leaves? an experiment

How the text works

● Watch the animation together and then talk about the subject matter (an experiment to see if geranium plants need leaves). Ask: *Who do you think it is for?* (School children of their own age.)

● Ask: *What is the text type?* (Instruction.) Invite the children to watch the animation again, listening carefully for features of instructional text, such as title to give purpose, list of things you need, sequence words (*Next, After several weeks*), commands (imperative tense), specific vocabulary (*as far as the 0mm line*).

● Discuss how the animation is different from written instructions, for example, oral instructions, sound effects (plucking of leaves), objects and steps shown visually.

● Talk about the expression and tones of the speaker. *What sort of person is it?* (For example: a teacher.) *Is the tone casual and friendly or more formal?* Discuss the pace of the narration. Look at sections of the animation together and find some pauses. Discuss their purpose.

● Talk about the benefits of an animation (more visuals to clarify instructions, more fun to watch) and a text (can easily refer back to it while doing the experiment). Ask: *Which would you find easier to follow if you wanted to do the experiment, and why?*

● Ask the children if they have seen an experiment on television or instructions on making something. *How does a broadcast with a camera differ from an animation?* Discuss how the animation is simpler and less cluttered, for example, you do not see the speaker or details of the setting. Discuss how some camera and animation techniques are similar, such as close-ups to zoom in on important details.

Responding to the text

- Prompt the children to recall a recent experiment they have done at school, or something they have made. Ask them to work in pairs, taking it in turns to give oral instructions on how to do it/make it. Remind them of the formal language used in the animation and the order in which the information is given (purpose, things you need, steps to take).

	Date	Plant A		Plant B (leaves removed)	
	Monday 9th	140mm	Healthy, lots of buds	145mm	Healthy,
Week 1	Monday 16th	145mm	Healthy, more leaves	135mm	No ... a few small buds gone
Week 2					
Week 3					

- Challenge the children to work out how they would turn the instructions in the animation into book text with just four illustrations. Tell them to work independently to write the instructions in as few words as possible and to pick and describe four simple illustrations that could appear alongside.

Writing activities

- Ask the children to work in small groups to plan a script for an animation that gives instructions on how to carry out an experiment or make something. Hand out photocopiable page 38 'Instructions' and demonstrate how to write an animation script, by working with the class on a possible opening:

[Narrator to sound like an enthusiastic scientist]

[Clear title text to appear: Instructions on how to measure the permeability of soil]

Narrator: In this experiment you will see how some soils are more permeable than others. You will need some clay-rich soil, some sandy soil [pause]

[Zoom in on the two different soils to show how their particle sizes and colours are different]

Narrator: two containers with small perforations at the bottom [show containers]

a measuring jug [show measuring jug]

a stopwatch [show stopwatch]

a pencil and paper. [show pencil and paper]

[pause]

Narrator: First, place one soil type in each container...

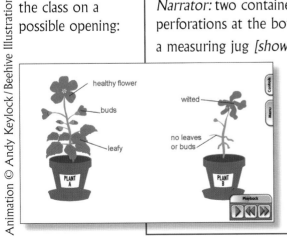

Assessment

- Does the children's script incorporate the essential information in a logical order?
- Do their visual instructions show an understanding of how graphics and narration work together in an animation?

Reference to 100 Literacy Framework Lessons

- Non-fiction Unit 2 Instructions pages 121–136

Photocopiable

- See page 38 or CD-ROM.

The Black Pearl

Objectives

● Strand 8: Empathise with characters and debate moral dilemmas portrayed in texts.
● Strand 9: Use layout, format, graphics and illustrations for different purposes.

Differentiation

Support
● Children draw four illustrations to tell their story. The illustrations should depict the beginning, middle and two alternative endings.
Extend
● The children can plan a third possible ending for their story.

Cross-curricular activities

ICT Unit 3A Combining text and graphics
● Ask the children to create a cover for the story they completed in the Writing activity, using various fonts, colours and graphics.

Whiteboard tools

● Whiteboard tools used on the screen shots include:
☁ Thought bubble
◒ Colour used ●

How the text works

● Read the first screen together. Talk about how it is similar to a book cover (title, author, illustration). Discuss the text and point out that it is like the 'blurb' on the back cover of a storybook.

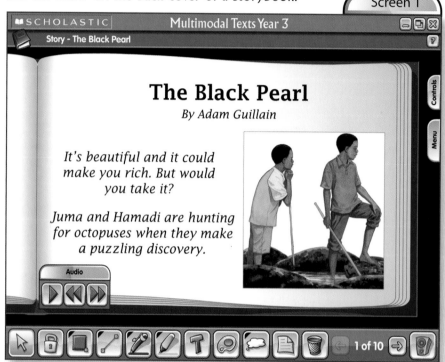

Screen 1

● Together read the next few screens, stopping at the end of screen 8. Ask the children to describe what sort of story it is. Encourage them to use the words 'adventure' or 'mystery'.

● Talk about how screen 8 is unlike most storybook pages (the reader is given two endings to choose from). Ask: *Can you buy books like this?* (Yes.) Invite children to describe any similar books they have read.

● Discuss the boys' dilemma and what they think each of the characters would prefer to do next, and why. Point out how Hamadi is more thoughtful and cautious on screen 7.

● Ask the class to explore both endings. Hold a class discussion on which is the most satisfying. Discuss how ending B is more dramatic, while ending A means we will never know if the pearl was magical.

● Invite the children to say whether they think a choice of endings is a good idea. Does this interactive element make it more exciting, or does it spoil the flow of the story?

Screen 5

● Review the setting of the story. Ask the children to identify words in the text that show the setting is not in this country (*clams, cassava, mchawi*). Encourage the children to name and describe relevant details in the illustrations, such as: palm trees, sandy beach with rocky outcrops and pools, no-one about except for the mchawi. Explain that the story is set on the Mombasa coast in East Africa and that *mchawi* is a local Kiswahili word that means 'wizard'.

■SCHOLASTIC
www.scholastic.co.uk

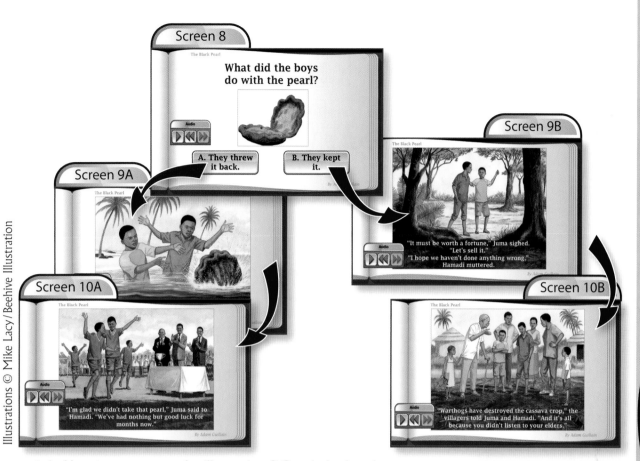

Illustrations © Mike Lacy / Beehive Illustration

• Ask: *How important are the illustrations?* Conclude that they are important in giving more information about the setting and the characters; in giving a sense of danger / mystery (the size and colour of the shell on screen 6, the mchawi walking away sadly on screen 7).

Responding to the text

• Review how the boys reacted differently throughout the story and in both endings. Ask: *Can you empathise with both boys?* Working as a class, write a thought bubble for each character on screens 3–6. Write thought bubbles for the illustrations in one ending too.

• Ask children to role play Hamadi and Juma each trying to persuade the other to throw the pearl back or take it. Then choose one ending and encourage the class to ask 'Hamadi' and 'Juma' how each of them felt. Repeat with the other ending.

• Recap on the importance of the illustrations. Ask the children to pick a screen and rewrite the text with details taken from the illustration. Ask volunteers to read out their text. Ask: *Is the text alone now enough?*

Writing activities

• Explain to the children that they are going to work in pairs to create a pictorial story with two endings, using narrative text, pictures and thought bubbles.

• Give photocopiable page 39 'A story with two endings' to each pair and discuss ways in which the children's stories can introduce a dilemma, leading to two possible endings, for example, two children find a diamond at school – what will they do with it?

• The children can use a digital camera (ensure you have parents' or carers' permission before taking photographs of children) or draw, scan and upload illustrations. The children can then construct their stories using presentation software.

Assessment

• Ask groups to swap stories and try out the different endings. Ask: *What is the dilemma? How do the characters' views differ? Are the characters convincing?*

Reference to *100 Literacy Framework Lessons*

• Narrative Unit 3 Adventure and mystery pages 48–51

Photocopiable

• See page 39 or CD-ROM.

SCHOLASTIC
www.scholastic.co.uk

Objective

● Strand 9: Use beginning, middle and end to write narratives in which events are sequenced logically and conflicts resolved.

Differentiation

Support
● Provide children with a simple book of a myth, legend or traditional story and ask them to read the story aloud, occasionally stopping for the rest of the group to mime important events.
Extend
● Children can present their story to the rest of the class, showing the photographs and reading their text aloud with expression.

Cross-curricular activities

Art and design Unit 3A
Portraying relationships
● Ask the children to sketch sequences of illustrations to show how the characters feel about each other at the beginning and end of the story, for example, the fearful widow begging the king who feels sorry for her; the widow thankful for the king's mercy.

The king who hated to have his hair cut

How the text works

● Recall and discuss some myths, legends or fables that the children are already familiar with. Explain that they are going to explore an illustrated Irish legend.

● Ask the children to read/listen to the story. Afterwards ask: *What does the story have in common with other myths or legends?* (For example: a powerful king, innocent people in danger.)

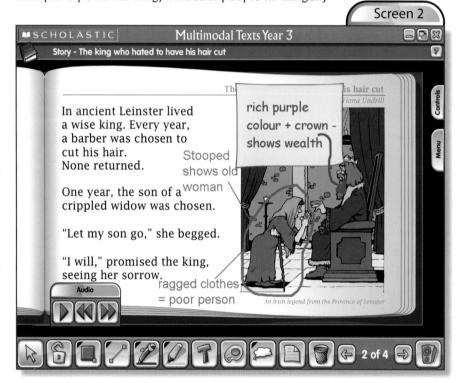

● Consider the plot structure. Ask the children to recall the beginning, then re-read the last screen. Discuss how the story is resolved. Ask: *Is it a happy ending for everyone? Why?*

● Discuss the choice of vocabulary and inclusion of illustrations. Ask: *Who is this story for? Is it for adults, children of their age or younger children?* Ask them to explain their views with reference to the text and illustrations.

● Discuss the character of the king, such as his strengths and weaknesses, the words that describe him and how he changes during the story.

● Encourage the children to refer to how the characters are portrayed in the illustrations. Would our view of the king be different if we could not see him in the illustrations? Does he look kind or cruel on screen 2?

● Discuss what else the illustrations contribute. What do they tell us about the setting? Do they create atmosphere or add humour? Would the story be as

■SCHOLASTIC
www.scholastic.co.uk

entertaining without them? Ask the children to highlight details in the pictures and label them with comments on the information they provide and/or mood they evoke.

- Together, listen to the story with eyes closed and discuss the way in which the reader narrates the dialogue. Ask: *Does the reader use a different voice for each character? Does the reader increase the pace, use pauses or vary the tone to create suspense? Is it an effective reading?*

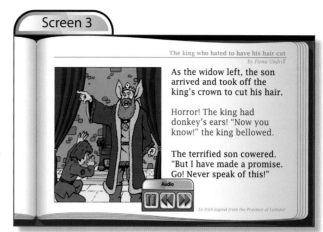

Screen 3

The king who hated to have his hair cut
by Fiona Undrill

As the widow left, the son arrived and took off the king's crown to cut his hair.

Horror! The king had donkey's ears! "Now you know!" the king bellowed.

The terrified son cowered. "But I have made a promise. Go! Never speak of this!"

An Irish legend from the Province of Leinster

Responding to the text

- Ask the children to work in pairs, and take turns to read the story aloud while the other listens and responds. Ask them to consider how the reading could be improved.

- Consider the action of the plot. Ask: *Could this be presented as a play or does it only work as a story with illustrations?* Ask the children to experiment by planning a simplified mimed or acted version of the play. Remind them to make sure that the beginning of the performance sets out the problem and the final scene resolves it.

Writing activities

- Explain to the children that you want them to work in small groups to retell a myth, legend or traditional story using a series of freeze-frame digital photographs. (Remember to get parents' or carers' permission before taking photographs of the children.) They can photograph group members miming the story. Provide props if possible.

- Hand out photocopiable page 40 'A story in photographs' to each group and ask them to use this to plan their visual version of the plot. Remind the children how illustrations in *The king who hated to have his hair cut* focused on the most important parts of the plot (the beginning, middle and end).

- After they have completed the photographs and uploaded them to the computer, ask them to write narrative text to go alongside each image using presentation software.

Whiteboard tools

- Whiteboard tools used on the screen shots include:
  - Line tool
  - Pen tool
  - Text tool
  - Sticky notes
  - Colours used ●●

Assessment

- Look at the stories the children produced in the Writing activity and consider whether or not the events are sequenced correctly, the stories have a clear beginning and end and essential details are included in the text.

Reference to *100 Literacy Framework Lessons*

- Narrative Unit 2 Myths and legends pages 25–44

Photocopiable

- See page 40 or CD-ROM.

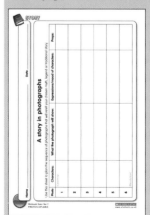

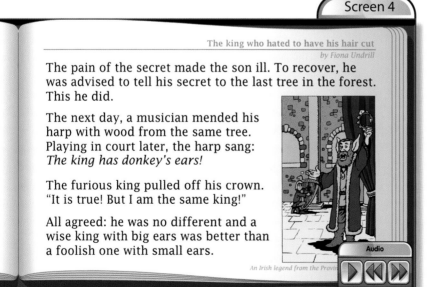

Screen 4

The king who hated to have his hair cut
by Fiona Undrill

The pain of the secret made the son ill. To recover, he was advised to tell his secret to the last tree in the forest. This he did.

The next day, a musician mended his harp with wood from the same tree. Playing in court later, the harp sang: *The king has donkey's ears!*

The furious king pulled off his crown. "It is true! But I am the same king!"

All agreed: he was no different and a wise king with big ears was better than a foolish one with small ears.

An Irish legend from the Provi...

Illustrations © Robin Edmonds/Beehive Illustration

Demeter and Persephone

Objectives

- Strand 4: Use some drama strategies to explore stories.
- Strand 10: Signal sequence, place and time to give coherence.

Differentiation

Support
- Children work on just the opening scene and dialogue between Demeter and Persephone, focusing on the setting before Hades appears.

Extend
- Children can extend their playscript to include the whole story, then perform it to others for comment.

Cross-curricular activities

ICT Unit 3A Combining text and graphics
- Create a visual dictionary on computer of Greek gods and goddess, adding their names, details and a scanned illustration. They can also add audio clips of each name being read aloud for pronunciation guidance.

Whiteboard tools

- Whiteboard tools used on the screen shots include:
  🖊 Pen tool
  T Text tool
  🔍 Colours used ●●

How the text works

- Read the story with the children. Afterwards ask: *What sort of story is this?* Identify it as a Greek myth and talk about other Greek myths they know. Ask: *What features do they have in common?* (For example: gods and goddesses, the Underworld, monsters, and heroes or heroines.)

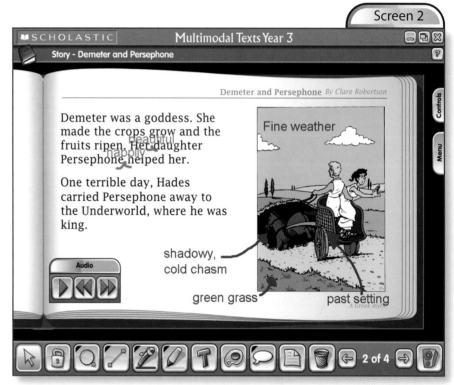

- Talk about the characters in the story. Ask: *What is Demeter the goddess of?* (The Harvest.) *Why is Zeus so powerful?* (He is king of the gods.) *Why did Hades take his new wife underground?* (He is god of the Underworld.)

- Ask the children to look at the illustration on screen 2. Ask: *What is its purpose?* Talk about the information it gives that is not found in the text, such as: blue sky suggests that the weather is fine, chariot and clothes show that the story is set in the past (Ancient Greece). Invite children to suggest descriptive labels for details, for example, 'green hills', 'green grass', 'shadowy, cold chasm'. Discuss how the details emphasise the dramatic difference between the two worlds and what they symbolise (life and death).

- Discuss the illustrations on screen 3. Talk about how the small inset illustration shows that Demeter is too late as Persephone has already eaten some seeds. Elicit how this emphasises the women's misfortune. Discuss the main illustration and how Zeus' power is depicted.

- Re-read screen 4. Discuss the language and whether it is descriptive. Ask the children to highlight descriptive words or phrases.

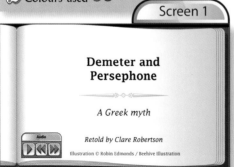

Demeter and Persephone

A Greek myth

Retold by Clare Robertson

Illustration © Robin Edmonds / Beehive Illustration

• Compare the illustrations on screen 4 and ask what additional information they give. Point out that the characters' feelings are not mentioned in the text, but are shown in the illustrations. Ask the children to describe how the characters are depicted in each illustration (lonely, isolated, cold; warm, happy).

Responding to the text

• Provide copies of the different screens, then ask the children to work independently and insert descriptive phrases into the text. Point out that they can use their imaginations as well as get ideas from the illustrations, for example, screen 2: *Her* beautiful *daughter Persephone* happily *helped her*; screen 3: *Zeus, King of the Gods, said* sadly... Discuss the children's ideas as a class and together choose the best words to insert on each screen. Invite volunteers to add them on the whiteboard. Ask children to read the new text aloud. Afterwards discuss whether or not the text still needs illustrations.

• Ask the children to work in pairs and compose a caption for each illustration. Discuss the usefulness of the captions as a class.

Writing activities

• Ask groups of four to prepare a playscript version of screen 2 of the story. Give out copies of photocopiable page 41 'A story for the stage' and ask them to plan each scene. Discuss how they will split the story into scenes, for example, Scene 1: Demeter and Persephone tending crops; Scene 2: Hades carries off Persephone. Explain that they will act out their script without using props and there will be no scenery, so important details and descriptions, about the setting, time and so on, must be in the speech. Talk through the first paragraph as an example, discussing how Demeter and Persephone can talk about the sunshine, meadow, ripening crops and fruit as they tend the crops together.

Screen 3

Demeter and Persephone By Clare Robertson

The corn wilted and the fruit dried on the trees, as Demeter cried for her daughter. She begged Zeus for help.

Zeus said, "Hades has taken Persephone to be his wife. As long as she eats nothing in the Underworld, she can be returned to you."

But Persephone had already eaten six tiny pomegranate seeds. When Zeus heard this, he ordered that Persephone must spend six months of every year in the dark of the Underworld. The other six she could spend with her mother.

Audio

Screen 4

Demeter and Persephone By Clare Robertson

And that is why, while Demeter waits for Persephone, the earth grows cold, the plants wither and die, and winter comes.

But when Persephone returns, so does the summer.

The sun shines and the plants grow once more.

Audio

A Greek myth

Assessment

• Ask groups to perform their opening scene of the story and discuss whether or not the settings are clear and the sequence of events are in a logical order.

Reference to *100 Literacy Framework Lessons*

• Narrative Unit 2 Myths and legends pages 25–44

Photocopiable

• See page 41 or CD-ROM.

A story for the stage

Illustrations © Robin Edmonds/Beehive Illustration

Barker!

Objective

● **Strand 4:** Present events and characters through dialogue to engage the interest of an audience.

Differentiation

Support
● Children write one simple scene in which the family are in the garden again, and Dad is pleased because the dog is not barking anymore.
Extend
● Groups rehearse their playscript and extra scenes, then record with sound effects. They can further edit the recording using computer software.

Cross-curricular activities

Citizenship Unit 3 Animals and us
● Ask the children to plan a playscript involving a child who faces a moral dilemma over his or her concerns about the welfare of a neighbour's pet.

How the text works

● Look at the playscript on the whiteboard together. Ask the children to highlight the features that show it is a playscript (such as: layout, scenes, directions for sound and speech). Ensure they understand the script features, prompt with questions such as: *What does Scene 1 mean? Why is* crossly *in brackets?*

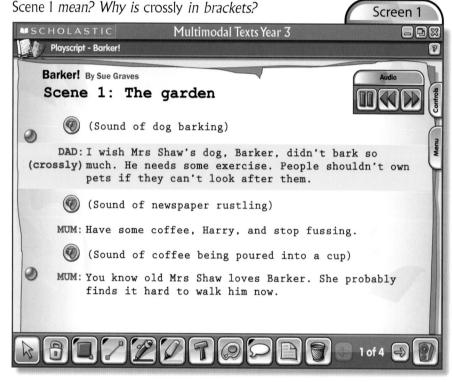

● Read the playscript with the children taking the roles, if appropriate include the sound effects. Afterwards, ask a volunteer to summarise the story. Discuss the characters and how they differ.

● Ask: *Could this script be used for a play on stage? If it was a script for stage or television, what else would it include?* (Stage directions, details of set.)

● Ask: *Is there enough information for the script to be performed as a radio play?* Discuss the sound directions and how these could be produced on a radio broadcast.

● Listen to the playscript with the children and ask them to compare it with their own reading. Discuss the use of sound and the expression, tone and volume of the characters' voices. Ask: *Did anything surprise you when you heard the characters? Did they sound as you expected? If not, why not?*

● Listen to the opening of the play and ask: *How much information do we get from listening to the first three spoken sentences?* Draw out the information (for example, the first sentence: Mrs Shaw has a dog that barks. The dog is called Barker. It makes the man cross. The voice tone suggests he is aged about 30–40 and is rather irritable). Emphasise how the dialogue moves the story on and the sound of the voices gives

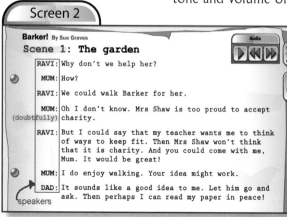

SCHOLASTIC
www.scholastic.co.uk

additional information.

- Consider the two settings. Ask: *What sound effects help us to imagine the details of the setting in Scene 1 and Scene 2?* (For example: the sound of pouring coffee gives an image of people seated at a table, a coffee pot, coffee and mugs.)

- Ask: *How did you feel at the start of Scene 2?* Talk about the effects of the barking and creaking door. Elicit how sound can create atmosphere and suspense.

Responding to the text

- Explain that the children should work in groups of four, so each group member can focus on one of the characters. Ask them to list the information they glean about the character from: what the character says, the sound of their voice, what they do, how others react to them or what others say about them. Encourage them to discuss their findings with their group.

- Ask: *How important is the tone, pace and expression of the voices?* Invite the children to work in groups to rehearse the play. Encourage them to think of any changes they might like to make from the original. Remind them to use expressive voices to portray their characters and to engage the listener. Ask them to record, listen to and revise their performance, or perform it to the others for feedback.

Writing activities

Explain that the children are going to work in groups of four to write two more scenes for the play. Discuss how the plot could be extended with another problem and resolution (for example: Ravi loses the dog, but it has run home).

Ask the children to use photocopiable page 42 'What happened next?' to plan each of their scenes. Remind them that everything must happen through dialogue and sound. When they are happy with their plan, they can type up and lay out their playscripts using *Barker!* as a model.

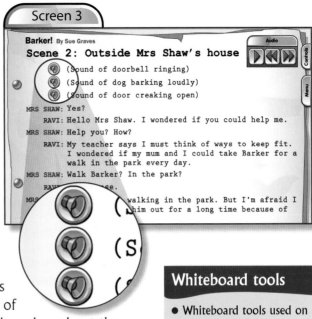

Screen 3

Barker! By Sue Graves

Scene 2: Outside Mrs Shaw's house

(Sound of doorbell ringing)
(Sound of dog barking loudly)
(Sound of door creaking open)

MRS SHAW: Yes?
RAVI: Hello Mrs Shaw. I wondered if you could help me.
MRS SHAW: Help you? How?
RAVI: My teacher says I must think of ways to keep fit. I wondered if my mum and I could take Barker for a walk in the park every day.
MRS SHAW: Walk Barker? In the park?

walking in the park. But I'm afraid I him out for a long time because of

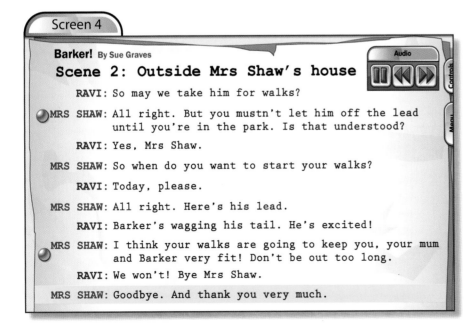

Screen 4

Barker! By Sue Graves

Scene 2: Outside Mrs Shaw's house

RAVI: So may we take him for walks?
MRS SHAW: All right. But you mustn't let him off the lead until you're in the park. Is that understood?
RAVI: Yes, Mrs Shaw.
MRS SHAW: So when do you want to start your walks?
RAVI: Today, please.
MRS SHAW: All right. Here's his lead.
RAVI: Barker's wagging his tail. He's excited!
MRS SHAW: I think your walks are going to keep you, your mum and Barker very fit! Don't be out too long.
RAVI: We won't! Bye Mrs Shaw.
MRS SHAW: Goodbye. And thank you very much.

Whiteboard tools

- Whiteboard tools used on the screen shots include:
  - Outline box
  - Pen tool
  - Highlighter
  - Text tool
  - Colours used ● ○

Assessment

- Invite groups to perform their two extra scenes to the class. Does the dialogue hold the listeners' attention? Are the characters still convincing? Is the dialogue spoken with expression?

Reference to *100 Literacy Framework Lessons*

- Narrative Unit 5 Dialogue and plays pages 83–100

Photocopiable

- See page 42 or CD-ROM.

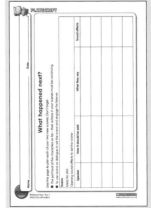

Voices

Illustration © Steve Millership / Beehive Illustration

Objectives

- Strand 1: Choose and prepare poems or stories for performance, identifying appropriate expression, tone, volume and use of voices and other sounds.
- Strand 8: Identify features that writers use to provoke readers' reactions.

Differentiation

Support
- Children can prepare just one verse for performance and work in groups of four so that each child reads one line.

Extend
- Groups can film their performances using a video recorder. (Remember to obtain parents' or carers' permission before filming the children.) They can use their recordings to assess and improve their reading.

Cross-curricular activities

ICT Unit 3B Manipulating sound
- The children create an audio recording, such as podcast, of a performance poem of their choice, using manipulated sound effects to enhance it.

Whiteboard tools

- Whiteboard tools used on the screen shots include:
- ○ Outline circle
- ＼ Line tool
- ✐ Highlighter
- T Text tool
- ◔ Colours used ○○●○○

How the text works

- Ask the children to read the first two verses, then listen to the poem. Discuss their initial reactions and talk about the features that are not found in a poetry book. Identify the various audio features: the speakers, music and sound effects.

- Listen to the first two verses again and ask the children to focus on the speakers' voices. Together consider the voice in each verse, how it varies and why. Prompt with questions such as: *In the second verse, why is the speaker's voice deep for the first line and high for the third line?* Remind the children of how some words can sound like the thing they are describing, such as *ding dong* sounds like a bell. Point out how the speakers emphasise these onomatopoeic words.

- Talk about the second verse illustrations. Elicit how the flowers are portrayed in ways that match the sound they make. Discuss which the children think are the most important, the illustrations or sound effects. Talk about how these features hold the attention and help the reader to understand the poem.

- Ask the children to read the rest of the verses. On the board, together note down the rhyming pattern in each verse. Elicit that the flower verses share the same rhyme scheme.

- Together, look for and mark

■SCHOLASTIC
www.scholastic.co.uk

alliterative words and phrases, (*Ding dong, 'Crack!' cries*).

- Introduce or revise the term 'performance poetry'. Discuss how it involves voice as well as text in engaging the audience, and how the audience of performance poems listen rather than read. Discuss the features that make poems effective performances (use of spoken words or sounds, strong rhythm, onomatopoeic words). Together identify the ways in which *Voices* is a performance poem.

Responding to the text

- On the board, together list the ways in which voices change: volume, pace, tone and expression. Ask the children to work in pairs and identify some of these changes in the voices on the audio. Ask them to label the text to show this. Alongside each verse ask them to list in order sounds they hear that are not a part of the text, such as speaker sighing, sound of bells. Ask the children to feed back their findings.

- Ask the children to work in groups of four and, reading a verse each, read the poem aloud, using expressive voices. Ask volunteers to perform to the class and ask for comments on what they think the speakers did well, and how the performance might be improved.

Writing activities

Ask the children to work in pairs to prepare a performance of *Voices*. Hand out photocopiable page 43 'Performing 'Voices'' and encourage them to use it to plan their performance carefully, they can also use it as a prompt when they perform to the rest of the class. Supply percussion instruments and sound-making equipment.

Assessment

- Ask groups to perform their poem or verse to the rest of the class. Discuss each performance constructively.
- Did the children use expressive voices, varying the tone, volume and pace?

Reference to *100 Literacy Framework Lessons*

- Poetry Unit 1 Poems to perform pages 157–167

Photocopiable

- See page 43 or CD-ROM.

Illustrations © Steve Millership/Beehive Illustration

Best Books

Objectives

- **Strand 1:** Choose and prepare poems or stories for performance, identifying appropriate expression, tone, volume and use of voices and other sounds.
- **Strand 2:** Identify the presentational features used to communicate the main points in a broadcast.

Differentiation

Support
- Encourage children to focus on the letters. After planning and writing their letters they can practise reading them aloud with expression.
Extend
- The children can record their script and, if possible, upload it to the school website as a podcast.

Cross-curricular activities

Citizenship Unit 2 Choices
- Ask the children to record their opinions for a podcast on children's views about an issue relevant to the class.

Whiteboard tools

- Whiteboard tools used on the screen shots include:
  - ✎ Line tool
  - ✐ Highlighter
  - ⊤ Text tool
  - ◉ Colour used ○

How the text works

- Ask volunteers to describe a podcast. If necessary, explain that a podcast is a broadcast that can be downloaded from the internet and on to computers and personal media players.

- Encourage the children to describe any podcasts they have listened to. Talk about how podcasts are aimed at all kinds of people and their content varies from interviews to pop music.

- Listen to the podcast. Afterwards, discuss the subject with the children. (Children's views on the best books to read.) Ask: *Who do you think the audience is, and why?* (Children of a similar age because of the informal language.) *What is the purpose of the text?* (To inform and persuade.)

- Listen to the opening again and ask: *Who are 'the kids in the know'?* (The presenters and perhaps other children involved in making of the podcast.) Discuss who else would be involved in making the broadcast, such as script writer, editor, production crew.

- Discuss how the letters are read. Ask questions such as: *Who reads the letters?* (The two presenters.) *Are the letters read with expression? Do you think the people who wrote the letters would be happy with how they were read?*

- Ask the children if it would be better to see and read the letters rather than listen to them. Discuss the benefits of hearing them (for example, enthusiasm in voices holds attention, music makes it more exciting). Discuss the benefits of printed letters (such as: easy to refer to later and take notes from, can take time to study and discuss).

- Look at the transcript together and talk about how the dialogue has been laid out. Ask the children to identify what would not be needed if it was printed text, such as a magazine page.

- Ask: *Do the letter writers' recommendations make you want to read any of the books? If so, why?* Discuss whether the podcast is persuasive. Revise the features of persuasive text. On the whiteboard identify persuasive features in the transcript such as strong adjectives and exaggeration (*great, Best book I've seen in ages!*).

- Compare the information in the letters with book reviews the children have written in the past. Do the letters and the children's reviews give a similar amount of information about the book and a similar number of reasons for recommending the book? Discuss which the class prefers and why.

Responding to the text

● If possible, source two or three suitable podcasts, such as interviews or sport reviews (copyright permitting) and ask the children to listen to them. As a class, compare their content, the presenters' voices and other features, such as music, with *Best Books*.

● Play the *Best Books* podcast again, this time ask the children to listen to it critically. In pairs, they should work together to create a list of ideas that would make the podcast more useful to someone who wants to decide which book really is 'the best'. Ask them to consider what additional information would be helpful (such as: more reasons why each book was enjoyed, information about the author, age of the letter writers, how the letters were chosen).

● Ask the children to role play the presenters and practise reading the text. Ask them to experiment with pace and tone. Encourage volunteers to present their reading to the class. Ask the class whether this was a better reading than the original.

Writing activities

● Explain that the children are going to work in groups of three to plan and write a script for a podcast in which they read their own letters describing their favourite books.

● Demonstrate how to write an audio script, by working with the class on a possible opening. Recall how the podcasts they listened to began (with music, for example). Refer the children to the transcript as you write the opening sound directions and speech.

● Each group member should then write a letter reviewing a favourite book using persuasive language. Ask the children to use the letters in the transcript as a model for their letter writing.

● Give photocopiable page 44 'Book review podcast' to each group. The group must work collaboratively and choose a group member to introduce and conclude the podcast. The group must also decide the order in which each individual reads out his or her letter.

Best Books

Dear Hannah and Alex,

I'm writing to tell you that the best book is: *The Wooden Mile* by Chris Mould, the first book in a series called *Something Wickedly Weird*. It's about a boy called Stanley Buggles who goes to a strange island and has to kill a werewolf! The story and pictures are great.
You should read it!

Yours sincerely
Ben Wilkinson

Assessment

● Ask the groups to present their scripts to the class and, if possible, include music or other sounds they had planned.
● Ask the children to discuss the content and presentation, for example: *Were the book reviews persuasive and informative? Were they read out with expression, pace and volume? Did the music contribute anything?*

Reference to *100 Literacy Framework Lessons*

● Narrative Unit 4 Authors and letters pages 65–82

Photocopiable

● See page 44 or CD-ROM.

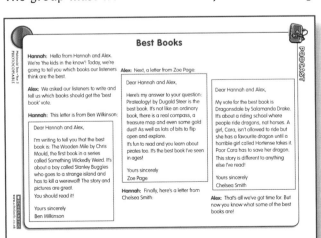

Mr Rot

Objectives

● **Strand 8:** Identify features that writers use to provoke readers' reactions.
● **Strand 9:** Use layout, format, graphics and illustrations for different purposes.

Differentiation

Support
● Children can focus on illustrations for a persuasive poster, plus a simple strap line.
Extend
● Children can adapt their poster and animate elements of it on-screen to create an eye-catching website advert.

Cross-curricular activities

Science Unit 3A
Teeth and eating
● Ask children to create an informative audio (with report and explanation text) describing a balanced diet and explaining its importance.

Whiteboard tools

● Whiteboard tools used on the screen shots include:
✎ Highlighter
◔ Colour used ●

How the text works

● Listen to the audio together, then discuss the subject (how to stop your teeth from rotting). Ask: *Who do you think the audio is for, and why?* (Children: child narrator, Mr Rot character and humour, reference to *sticky sweets*.)

● Invite the children to describe similar broadcasts, such as adverts, that they have heard on the radio or seen on television. Discuss how radio and television advertisements differ. Elicit how a television advert can be even more powerful as it targets two of the viewer's senses (sight and hearing) instead of one.

● Ask: *What text type is used?* Elicit that it is persuasive text. Look at the transcript of the audio together and ask volunteers to highlight persuasive language features, such as strong positive language (*Stop Mr Rot*), alliterations (*teeth, twice, nasty, sticky sweets*). Discuss how the advert also provides evidence and information to persuade you.

● Discuss the mood of the advert. *What is the purpose of the sound effects and the character of Mr Rot?* Talk about how the humour might draw children in, and how the dramatic sounds grab the listener's attention. Ask if an advert like this is more memorable, and why (it puts images in your mind, the character adds interest).

● Discuss the different voices. Compare what is said by the child and what is said by the narrator. Elicit how the adult voice emphasises the seriousness of tooth decay and the importance of what you should do to look after your teeth.

● Listen to the audio, stopping it occasionally so that children can write down the words and phrases that are emphasised. Ask: *Why are these emphasised?* Discuss the change in volume, tone and expression in the voices.

Responding to the text

● Ask the children to work in pairs and role play a parent and child dialogue in which the parent is trying to persuade their child to look after their teeth. Try out and discuss different methods of persuasion, for example, frightening the child (could it give the child nightmares?), giving the child information and evidence (the child can then make an informed decision).

● Encourage the children to think about why the slogan *Stop Mr Rot* is effective. Ask them to work in groups and brainstorm other ideas for slogans that could be used to persuade people to look after their teeth.

● Play the audio again and ask the children to listen to it critically. Ask them to work in small groups to come up with a list of ideas that would make the audio more persuasive, such as facts from a dentist, horrible descriptions on what rot looks like and the possible consequences of rot, witness accounts of toothache, more sound effects (dentist's drill), rhetorical questions and so on.

Writing activities

● Hand out photocopiable page 45 'A persuasive poster' and ask the children to use it to plan a poster persuading children to look after their teeth. Explain that their poster can include material from the audio. Suggest, however, that they add ideas of their own and remind them of the previous exercise in which they listened to the audio critically. Point out that there will be little room for text, so persuasive slogans and eye-catching, colourful illustrations are important.

● After planning their poster ask the children to put it together using appropriate computer software. Print the posters out and ask the children to seek feedback from their friends.

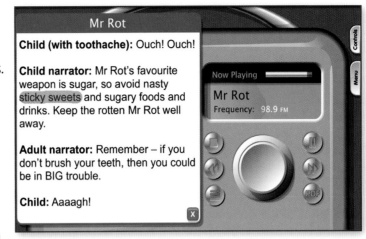

Mr Rot

Child (with toothache): Ouch! Ouch!

Child narrator: Mr Rot's favourite weapon is sugar, so avoid nasty sticky sweets and sugary foods and drinks. Keep the rotten Mr Rot well away.

Adult narrator: Remember – if you don't brush your teeth, then you could be in BIG trouble.

Child: Aaaagh!

Now Playing
Mr Rot
Frequency: 98.9 FM

Assessment

● Do the children use persuasive language and visual features effectively in their adverts?
● Do they include evidence to back up their point?
● Do they include features from the audio, such as alliteration, humour or drama, and a slogan?

Reference to *100 Literacy Framework Lessons*

● Non-fiction Unit 3 Information texts pages 144–146

Photocopiable

● See page 45 or CD-ROM.

Mr Rot

Child:	Aaaagh!
Child narrator:	Stop Mr Rot from getting at your teeth. Keep the plaque away by brushing your teeth, twice a day.
Adult narrator:	Plaque causes tooth decay, so you need to brush it away. Don't forget – brush your teeth after breakfast and just before you go to bed.
Child narrator:	Stop Mr Rot from getting at your teeth. If you let Mr Rot in, you could get toothache.
Child (with toothache):	Ouch! Ouch!
Child narrator:	Mr Rot's favourite weapon is sugar, so avoid nasty sticky sweets and sugary foods and drinks. Keep the rotten Mr Rot well away.
Adult narrator:	Remember – if you don't brush your teeth, then you could be in BIG trouble.
Child:	Aaaagh!

Shadows

Objective

● **Strand 9:** Use beginning, middle and end to write narratives in which events are sequenced logically and conflicts resolved.

Differentiation

Support
● Children can draw four illustrations representing their storyboard. Remind them to use contrasting light/dark colours for dramatic effect.
Extend
● Children can extend their storyboard on computer into a multi-image story with captions and speech bubbles, similar to a comic, but with sound effects.

Cross-curricular activities

Science Unit 3F Sunlight and shadows
● Using a digital camera to create a display of interesting shadow shapes made by sunlight and/or a torch. Display as a visual quiz, entitled 'What made this shadow shape?'

How the text works

● Look at the first image with the children. Explain that it is one of four pictures that together tell a short story. Discuss the possible age of the two characters, their likely relationship and the setting. Ask: *Have you ever shone a torch under your face?* Talk about the sound effect and what it adds (drama/sense of surprise). *Does the image make you want to see more? Is it a good beginning to a story? If so, why?*

● Look at the second image and ask children to summarise the story so far. Ask: *Do you think the illustrations and sound effects are enough to tell the story? Would it be easier to understand if there were captions?*

● Look at the third image and consider the sound effect. Ask: *Does the sound effect add to the story? Does it make you want to know what happens next?*

● Discuss the children's feelings towards the main character at this point. Ask: *Do you think he is taking things too far? How would you feel if you were his brother, sister or dog? What might happen next?*

● View the final image and discuss whether it was a satisfactory ending. (The little brother scares him.) Does the story have a message? What was the 'conflict' in the story and how was it resolved?

● Ask: *Do you think it was right that the boy should get a 'taste of his own medicine'?* Talk about other stories the children are familiar with that include someone 'getting their own back'. Discuss other ways in which the family could have reacted, such as taking his torch away.

SCHOLASTIC
www.scholastic.co.uk

• Together, look at the images again but without listening to the sounds. Ask: *Is the story understandable? Does it hold your attention so well without the sound?* Discuss how the sound effects are dramatic, how they hold the attention and create atmosphere.

• Look through the illustrations and compare: the angles of view, whether the images are close-ups, how light / dark is used. Point out how close-ups / angles of view can be more dramatic, adding variety to the sequence and changing the viewpoint.

Responding to the text

• Ask the children to work in pairs to take turns to narrate the story. For each image, the narrator uses story language to say what happens, for example, 'One day Harry took out his torch and thought, "I think I'll pay a joke on Tom."'

• In pairs, ask the children to compose speech bubbles for Tom in the first three images and for the little brother in the fourth.

Writing activities

• Ask groups of four to prepare a photo storyboard. Give a copy of photocopiable page 46 'A shadowy tale' to each group. Explain that before filling out the sheet they must plan the plot for a story, if possible involving a 'shadow' theme. Explain that they will take the photographs using a digital camera. The images can be of the children in role (get parents' or carers' permission before taking photographs) or of small-word figures or toys. The children can upload the photographs to the computer and add sound effects or music to each.

• After they are completed, the groups can swap their storyboards. Each group can then write a narrative for another group's story. Are the narratives as the storyboard-makers intended? Share the results in class.

Whiteboard tools

• Whiteboard tools used on the screen shots include:
Speech bubble
Colour used ●

Assessment

• Do the children use the camera effectively? Does their story have a logical sequence with a clear beginning and a satisfying end?

Reference to *100 Literacy Framework Lessons*

• Narrative Unit 2 Stories with familiar settings pages 9–24

Photocopiable

• See page 46 or CD-ROM.

Weather around the world

Objective

● Strand 1: Explain process or present information, ensuring that items are clearly sequenced, relevant details are included and accounts are ended effectively.

Differentiation

Support
● Children prepare and perform a talk on one of the locations only, saying why it is a good place to go on holiday.
Extend
● Children can extend their presentations to create a multimedia book on 'Weather around the world'.

Cross-curricular activities

Geography Unit 10 A village in India
● Ask children to plan a presentation on how the weather, such as monsoon rain, affects life in a location in India.

How the text works

● Ask the children to look at the sequence of images and listen to the sound effects. Ask what they have in common and elicit that they all show a weather-type commonly found in certain parts of the world.

● Discuss where you might find photographs like these, such as geography books, books on weather/climate, travel books, travel brochures or the internet.

Screen 1

● Discuss the sound effects and ask: *What do they add to the pictures?* (They give you a sense of being there; they emphasise the weather and landscape featured.)

● Look at picture 1 together and ask: *What clues are there about the weather?* (Wet ground, droplets on camera lens, sound effect suggests lots of rain.) *What clues are there about the environment?* Elicit that this is a mountainside somewhere like Great Britain.

Screen 2

The snow is soft and deep here

● Move on to picture 2, discussing it as above. Point out the person's clothing and elicit that it shows how cold and remote the environment is. Discuss how snow is often found on high mountains.

● Look at picture 3. Ask children to point to and label all the visual clues they can find that the weather is hot and that the environment is a desert (cloudless sky, people in shorts, camels, dry-looking land, no rivers, no plants).

• Look at picture 4 together and ask: *What clues are there about the weather?* (Wet ground suggests lots of rain.) *What clues are there about the environment?* Elicit that this is a rainforest. Talk about why a rainforest and heavy rain are linked. Ask: *What does the sound effect tell us?* (Rainforests are home to many animals.)

Responding to the text

• Together write thought bubbles for one character in each photo, focusing on their possible thoughts about the weather / environment, for example 'The snow is soft and deep here.' Discuss what the pictures would be like without the people, for example, we would lose a sense of the size of the landscape, it would be harder to imagine what the weather feels like to a human being. Ask the children to decide in small groups which photograph and sound effect is (i) the most dramatic, (ii) the most informative about the weather and environment. Ask them to explain their choices with reference to, for example, the camera angles and long- or short-distance shots.

• Ask the children to work independently. Encourage half the class to imagine that the photographs are in a book about 'world weather' and to write a caption for each photo that includes relevant details. Ask the other half to imagine the photographs are in a holiday brochure and to write a caption that includes details that would interest holidaymakers. Compare some of the children's captions.

Writing activities

• Ask groups of four to create a presentation, using presentation software, entitled 'What will the weather be like?' Explain that their presentation is for travellers who are choosing a destination for an 'adventure' holiday and who want to know what the weather and environment will be like in four popular destinations. The presentation will be spoken and supported by the on-screen presentation. Ask the groups to use photocopiable page 47 'What will the weather be like?' to plan their presentation. Explain that they need to write what they will say, and source the picture for each destination (for example, clip art or scanned artwork of their own). Each group member could research, prepare and present information on one of the destinations.

Whiteboard tools

• Whiteboard tools used on the screen shots include:
Speech bubble
Colour used ●

Assessment

• Ask groups to perform their presentations. Observe the following points: Have they organised the information logically? Do they include relevant information? Do they have a concluding speech at the end?

Reference to *100 Literacy Framework Lessons*

• Non-fiction Unit 1 Reports pages 101–120

Photocopiable

• See page 47 or CD-ROM.

IMAGES

Name _____ **Date** _____

Book page plan

Plan your pages on Hadrian's Villa and the Roman baths in Bath carefully.
Remember to consider the following:

● Text (what to include).

● Visual elements, including labels and captions.

● Layout features: font; additional graphics; colours.

Write a heading for each paragraph and notes for what it will contain.

Paragraph 1: _____

_____

Paragraph 2: _____

_____

Paragraph 3: _____

_____

List two illustrations and their captions or labels.

1 _____

_____

2 _____

_____

Ideas for layout

Fonts (size, style)

Headings: _____

Main text: _____

Captions/labels _____

Other graphics, such as background colours _____

_____

Name _____ **Date** _____

How to... Where to buy...

Use this page to plan your website. For each page consider:
- Audience and purpose.
- The text type.
- Visuals (pictures, diagrams, fonts, colours, graphics).
- Links to web pages or websites.

Page 1 How to... _____

Website address: www. _____

Text: _____

_____

Illustrations: _____

Design ideas: _____

Content of advert for selling website: _____

_____

> **Linking word/button to selling website**

Page 2 Website address: www. _____

Menu of links to other pages on the website:

_____

_____

_____

_____

Linking words/ buttons to checkout

Text: _____

_____

_____

Illustrations: _____

_____

Design ideas: _____

_____

Name _____ Date _____

Extreme weather website

● Use this page to plan your website on extreme weather.

Page 1 Website address: www. _____

Information on this page (text and visuals): _____

_____

Design ideas: _____

Links to other websites/pages: _____

Linking word/button

Page 2 Website address: www. _____

Information on this page (text and visuals): _____

_____

Design ideas: _____

Links to other websites/pages: _____

Linking word/button

Page 3 Website address: www. _____

Information on this page (text and visuals): _____

_____

Design ideas: _____

Links to other websites/pages: _____

_____

Name _____   Date _____

My day at school

Use this sheet to plan your 'day at school' film. Continue on another sheet if you need more than four scenes.

	What the camera sees	What the narrator says	Sound effects
Scene 1: Arriving at school			
Scene 2:			
Scene 3:			
Scene 4:			

 **ANIMATION**

Name _____ Date _____

Instructions

Use this page to plan your script. Remember to check that any visuals or sound effects clarify the narrated instructions.

Remember to write text that is easy to read aloud.

Title: _____

Introduction (purpose of the instructions):

Spoken text: _____

_____

Ideas for visuals/sound effects _____

What you need:

Spoken text: _____

_____

Ideas for visuals/sound effects _____

Sequence of steps: **Ideas for visuals/
                                                           sound effects:**

1 _____   _____

_____   _____

2 _____   _____

_____   _____

3 _____   _____

_____   _____

4 _____   _____

_____   _____

5 _____   _____

_____   _____

(Continue on another sheet if necessary.)

Multimodal Texts • Year 3
PHOTOCOPIABLE

SCHOLASTIC
www.scholastic.co.uk

Name _____ **Date** _____

A story with two endings

Use this page to plan your story and illustrations. Remember that the story must lead to a dilemma and two possible endings.

Picture 1:

What will the picture show? _____

Speech/thought bubble: _____

Text: _____

Picture 2:

What will the picture show? _____

Speech/thought bubble: _____

Text: _____

Picture 3:

What will the picture show? _____

Speech/thought bubble: _____

Text: _____

Picture 4:

What will the picture show? _____

Speech/thought bubble: _____

Text: _____

Ending A What will the picture show?	**Ending B** What will the picture show?
_____	_____
Speech/thought bubble: _____	Speech/thought bubble: _____
_____	_____
Text: _____	Text: _____
_____	_____

■SCHOLASTIC
www.scholastic.co.uk

Name _____

Date _____

A story in photographs

Use this sheet to plan the sequence of photographs that will retell your chosen myth, legend or traditional story.

Photo	Characters:	What the photograph will show:	Expressions/mood of characters:	Props:
1	(Opening)			
2				
3				
4				
5				
6	(Resolution)			

Multimodal Texts • Year 3
PHOTOCOPIABLE

Name _____   **Date** _____

A story for the stage

Use this page to plan your playscript. Continue on another sheet if necessary.

Don't forget:

● The characters must be convincing.

● Information about the setting and time must be given through the dialogue.

● The audience must be engaged (for example, they should feel sorry for the main characters).

Scene		
Stage directions	**Name of the speaker**	**What they say (how they say it)**

Name _____ Date _____

What happened next?

Use this page to plan each of your two new scenes. Don't forget:

● The portrayal of the characters so far – their actions in your scenes must be convincing.

● To use sound or dialogue to set the scene and engage the listener.

Scene

Ideas for plot:

Opening sound effects to set the scene:

Speaker	How it should be said	What they say	Sound effects

Multimodal Texts • Year 3
PHOTOCOPIABLE

SCHOLASTIC
www.scholastic.co.uk

Name _____   Date _____

Performing 'Voices'

Use this page to plan your performance.

● Annotate each line of the poem with ideas for variations in your voices. An example has been done for you.

● List your sound effects in the column on the right.

● Remember the importance of using volume, pace, tone and expression to engage the audience.

● Choose how to divide the reading between your group members.

sound out like a cow

Cows moo: that's nothing new;
Horses say, 'Neigh!'
Dogs woof; cats mew;
But what do flowers say?

'Boing!' trills the daffodil,
Calling in the spring;
'Ding dong, ding dong,'
The bluebells sing.

'Crack!' cries the snapdragon;
'Sniff!' goes the rose;
'Me, me, me!' forget-me-nots
Are whispering at your toes.

But, in the autumn showers,
Before the flowers die,
If you listen carefully
You'll hear their petals sigh.

Celia Warren

Sound effects:

_____
_____
_____
_____
_____
_____
_____
_____
_____
_____
_____

Name _____ **Date** _____

Book review podcast

Use this page to plan your podcast. Remember to consider both the content of the text and how it will sound when you read it out. Remember to write text that is easy to read with expression.

The **group's name**, such as 'The Book Guzzlers':

_____

Name of the **main presenter**: _____
What the presenter will say:

Introduction: _____

_____

_____

_____

_____

Conclusion: _____

_____

_____

_____

_____

Order in which letters will be read:

Reader	**Book title**
1: _____	_____
2: _____	_____
3: _____	_____

Ideas for **other sounds**, such as music: _____

_____

_____

AUDIO

Name _____ **Date** _____

A persuasive poster

Use this sheet to brainstorm ideas and plan your poster.

Remember:

● Make every word count towards persuading the reader.

● Visuals should be eye-catching and memorable as well as persuasive.

The purpose of the poster

To persuade children to _____

Evidence/reasons why they should do as you say:

● _____

● _____

● _____

● _____

● _____

Ideas for…

Slogans: _____

Alliterative phrases: _____

Rhetorical questions: _____

Characters (like Mr Rot): _____

Ideas for visuals:

Font style and colour _____

Images, such as cartoon characters _____

_____

Other graphics, such as background colour _____

_____

SCHOLASTIC
www.scholastic.co.uk

Name _____   Date _____

A shadowy tale

Use this page to plan your photograph storyboard. Don't forget to plan your plot first and have a clear beginning, middle and end.

Photograph 1	Photograph 2
Content: _____	Content: _____
_____	_____
_____	_____
_____	_____
Ideas for angle of view and so on:	Ideas for angle of view and so on:
_____	_____
_____	_____
Sound effects: _____	Sound effects: _____
_____	_____
Photograph 3	**Photograph 4**
Content: _____	Content: _____
_____	_____
_____	_____
_____	_____
Ideas for angle of view and so on:	Ideas for angle of view and so on:
_____	_____
_____	_____
Sound effects: _____	Sound effects: _____
_____	_____

Multimodal Texts • Year 3
PHOTOCOPIABLE

Name _____ **Date** _____

What will the weather be like?

Use this page to plan your presentation on four 'adventure' holiday destinations. You may want to include extra visual information, such as an introductory map, to show where the destinations are.

Introduction		
Speaker:	What will you say?	Content of visual

Main section		
Picture title	What will you say…	
	…about the location/ environment/adventure activity?	…about the weather?
1		
2		
3		
4		

Ending	
Speaker:	What you will say…

SCHOLASTIC

Also available in this series:

ISBN 978-0439-94577-6

ISBN 978-1407-10013-5

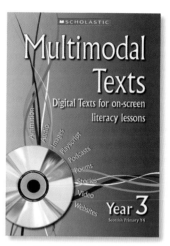

ISBN 978-1407-10014-2

ISBN 978-1407-10015-9

ISBN 978-1407-10016-6

ISBN 978-1407-10017-3

To find out more, call: 0845 603 9091
or visit our website www.scholastic.co.uk